The Oregon Trail

Westward Ho!

by Louise Orlando

Table of Contents

Introduction 2

Chapter 1
Why People Headed West 4

Chapter 2
Westward Ho! 8

Chapter 3
A Proud Pioneer 12

Chapter 4
The Trail Today 14

Conclusion 18

Glossary and Index 19

Comprehension Check 20

Introduction

Picture this. You are 10 years old. When you get home from school, your parents have some news. Your family is moving all the way across the country to Oregon. Most of your family's things are packed in a wagon. You are about to leave on the longest journey of your life.

In the 1840s, thousands of people left their homes in the East. They headed west to places such as Oregon and California. These people were called **pioneers**. They wanted land for farms and ranches. Some of them hoped to find gold. Everyone wanted to make their lives better.

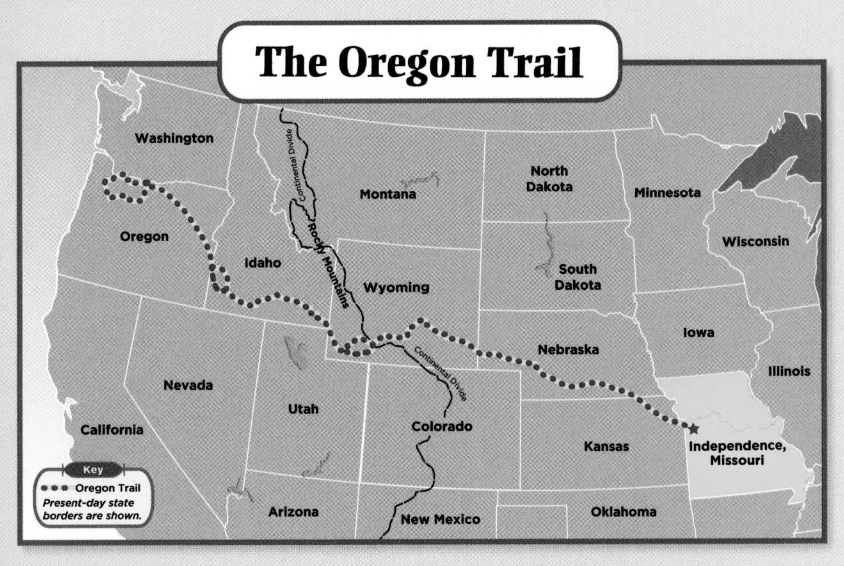

The Oregon Trail began in Independence, Missouri. It took four to six months to go from Missouri to Oregon.

At the time, there were no cars or planes. Trains didn't cross the country yet. Most people headed west following a route called the Oregon Trail. Over half a million dedicated people traveled over the trail. They made the **trek** over 2,000 dusty, bumpy, wet, hot, and freezing miles. Those who traveled the Oregon Trail became an important part of history. Today, many tourists revisit the trail to follow the paths of those brave pioneers.

Between 1840 and 1860, over 300,000 people traveled west on the Oregon Trail.

CHAPTER 1

Why People Headed West

Before the Oregon Trail, the only way for settlers to reach the west coast was to take a long journey by boat. People had been looking for an easier route west for many years.

In 1804, President Thomas Jefferson sent Meriwether Lewis and William Clark to explore the land west of the Mississippi. He hoped that the explorers would find an easy overland route to the Pacific Ocean.

Lewis and Clark spent two years exploring the West, charting the rivers and creating maps of the land.

This is what South Pass looks like today.

Lewis and Clark found a way across the Rocky Mountains and reached the Pacific Ocean. But the path was too dangerous for settlers and their wagons. People had to keep searching for a land route.

John Astor was a businessman. He wanted to build his fur-trading business in the West. But his trappers needed a better route. So Astor secretly paid a group to find a route west.

The group discovered a 20-mile gap in the Rocky Mountains. Wagons would be able to cross the mountains through this gap. The gap was later named South **Pass**. It became the main route west.

Then in 1848, a discovery made the route very important. Gold had been found in California. It didn't take long for people to catch gold "fever." As many as 30,000 people may have moved west in 1849. They were hoping to find land—with gold on it.

But it was not only gold that caused people to go west. Many people saw the West as a land of opportunity. In the East, farms were small, and the land was often not good for farming. Farmland in the West was cheap, and there was lots of it. So hundreds of thousands joined the many wagon trains leaving for the Oregon Territory.

First, the settlers made their way to Independence, Missouri. It was the "jumping off point" for the trip. People from all over the East arrived there. Some had wagons or carts. In Independence, they bought supplies. Then they joined other groups of pioneers trekking west. They formed wagon trains. Scouts rode ahead of the trains to make sure the path was safe.

Eagle Rock in Nebraska was one of ➲ the landmarks settlers looked for.

CHAPTER 2

Westward Ho!

Imagine walking 2,000 miles on the Oregon Trail. Most pioneers did it in about six months. Why didn't they ride in the wagons? Most of the wagons were packed so full that there wasn't room. Also, many people couldn't afford wagons. They pushed or pulled carts the entire way.

Although thousands headed west, not all of them made it. An illness called **cholera** killed many people. Some died accidentally. Others waited too long to start their journey, and winter overtook them.

William (John) Livingston ➲ was one of the pioneers who traveled west on the Oregon Trail.

One such group was the Donner party. In 1846, the Donner and Reed families joined a wagon train in Independence, Missouri. The wagon train was headed to California. On the way, the train met travelers from the West who urged them to take a different route. The travelers said the path the wagon train was on would become too difficult. It was too close to winter.

The First Pioneers

Marcus and Narcissa Whitman and Henry and Eliza Spaulding were the first pioneers to make the journey to Oregon successfully. Narcissa and Eliza were the first white women to complete the Oregon Trail. They opened the way for thousands of other women, who hoped to find more equality and freedom in the West.

The Donners and Reeds didn't listen to the warning. They left the wagon train and continued on the path. They believed it would save them hundreds of miles.

The Donners and the Reeds had made a terrible mistake. The path they had chosen was much more difficult and longer. The families were forced to spend the winter in the Sierra Nevada Mountains. Winters in these mountains are harsh. But the winter of 1846–1847 was one of the worst winters in recorded history. The families' food quickly ran out. Many froze to death. Out of 87 people, only 46 lived.

Today, cars travel on the path that the Donners and the Reeds took. It is now a paved road that is open all year round.

In the Words of Tamsen Donner

"June 16th. We are now on the Platte [River], 200 miles from Fort Laramie. I never could have believed we could have traveled so far with so little difficulty. Indeed, if I do not experience something far worse than I have yet done, I shall say the trouble is all in getting started."

Tamsen died that winter in the Sierra Nevada Mountains.

Chapter 3

A Proud Pioneer

As the population grew in the West, people needed a faster way to travel and ship goods across the country. In 1869 the transcontinental railroad was completed. It was the first railroad to join the eastern and western parts of the country. People began to travel west by train. Soon, the Oregon Trail was almost forgotten. But one man vividly remembered the Oregon Trail. His name was Ezra Meeker.

Workers cheer the first train over the Sierra Nevada Mountains.

In 1852, Ezra Meeker and his family traveled on the Oregon Trail. Meeker arrived in Oregon amazed and thrilled that they had made it. He and his family settled in Washington Territory. He lived there quietly for 50 years, but his memories of the trail remained alive.

Meeker decided to do something to make sure that people did not forget about the Oregon Trail. In 1906 he traveled the trail again in a wagon. On his journey, he stopped and spoke about the trail. He marked various locations that he remembered. This trip proved to be the first of many. Meeker traveled the trail by wagon, car, train, and finally airplane. Thanks to Ezra Meeker, many of the **landmarks** and artifacts of the Oregon Trail have been preserved.

Ezra Meeker wrote a book ➲ about his many journeys on the Oregon Trail.

Chapter 4

The Trail Today

Many pioneers made their way along the Oregon Trail by following landmarks. Forts were among the most important of these landmarks. They acted as supply and rest stations and can be visited.

Other landmarks were small towns along the trail and sites where people long ago discovered gold or silver. Along the trail, you can still see ruts that wagon wheels wore into the trail. You can also see the graves of those who didn't survive the journey.

Chimney Rock, Nebraska

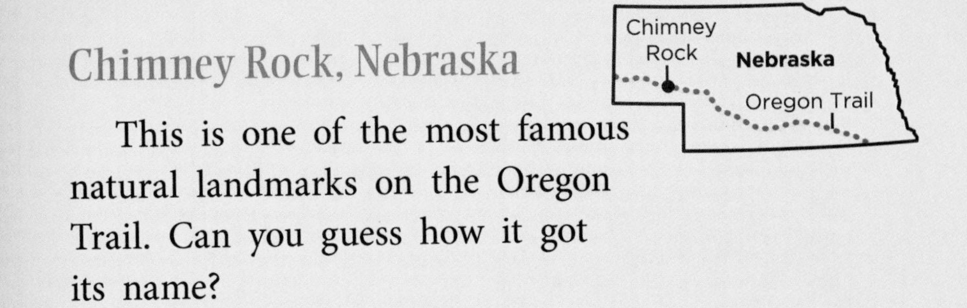

This is one of the most famous natural landmarks on the Oregon Trail. Can you guess how it got its name?

South Pass, Wyoming

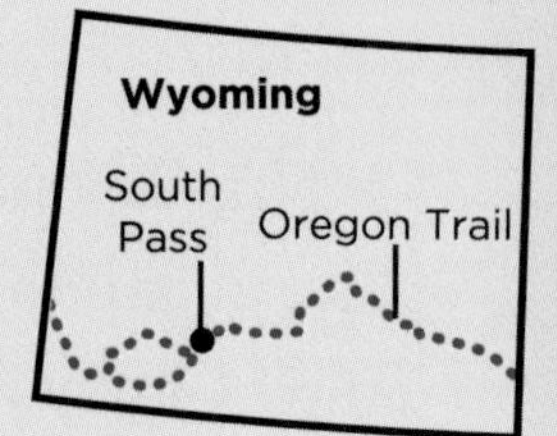

This might be the most important landmark on the trail. It was the way through the Rocky Mountains. In 1867, gold was discovered in South Pass. South Pass City quickly sprang up.

Three Island Crossing, Idaho

Pioneers used these three islands as "stepping stones" to cross the Snake River. Once a year, people dress in costumes and pretend to be pioneers. They drive wagons, horses, and oxen across the river.

Whitman Mission, Washington

Parts of the mission built by Marcus and Narcissa Whitman still stand here.

Oregon City, Oregon

This marked the end of the trail for most pioneers.

Oregon City was a booming city in the 1850s.

Conclusion

The 2,000-mile Oregon Trail was not an easy trip in the 1800s. And it's not an easy trip today, either. Think about those pioneers. They went west in search of new lives. They hoped to find opportunities. If not for them, Oregon, California, Washington, Nevada, Idaho, and Utah might not be part of the United States today.

Today we can take short or long hikes along the Oregon Trail. We can stop and enjoy the view. We can have lunch and camp out. But most of all, we can take the time to really think about the hardships many of those pioneers faced.

Tourists visit exhibits about the Oregon Trail here.

Glossary

cholera *(KOL-ur-uh)* an illness that can cause death ***(page 8)***

landmark *(LAND-mahrk)* an object or structure that can serve as a guide ***(page 13)***

pass *(PAS)* a gap or passage in a mountain range ***(page 5)***

pioneer *(pigh-uh-NEER)* a person who is among the first to explore and settle a region ***(page 2)***

trek *(TREK)* a long and difficult journey ***(page 3)***

Index

Astor, John, *5*

California Gold Rush, *6*

Chimney Rock, Nebraska, *15*

Clark, William, *4–5*

Donner family, *9–11*

forts, *14*

Independence, Missouri, *3, 6*

Lewis, Meriwether, *4–5*

Meeker, Ezra, *12–13*

Oregon City, *17*

Rocky Mountains, *5, 16*

Sierra Nevada Mountains, *10*

South Pass, Wyoming, *5, 16*

Three Island Crossing, Idaho, *16*

transcontinental railroad, *12*

Whitman, Narcissa and Marcus, *9, 17*

Comprehension Check

Summarize

Retell *The Oregon Trail: Westward Ho!* What are three important events in the history of the Oregon Trail? Why is it an important part of American history?

Think and Compare

1. Look back at pages 12–13. Why are people such as Ezra Meeker important? Why did he feel it was important to travel the Oregon Trail so many times? ***(Identify Main Idea and Details)***

2. Would you like to travel the 2,000 miles of the Oregon Trail today? Explain your reasons. ***(Apply)***

3. Many places along the Oregon Trail are now national parks. Do you think it's good to preserve these landmarks? Name other places you think should be protected. Give reasons for your answer. ***(Evaluate)***